NOV 0 1

WELLESLEY FREE LIBRARY

W9-BVN-240

WELLESLEY FREE LIBRARY
WELLESLEY, MASS. 02482

Come Out and Play

Maya Ajmera • John D. Ivanko

*with a foreword by **Kermit the Frog***

SHAKTI for Children
Charlesbridge

WELLESLEY FREE LIBRARY
WELLESLEY, MASS. 02482

JUVENILE
790
Ajmera

HI-HO!

It's Kermit the Frog here. Looking at the beautiful pictures in this book brings back wonderful memories of when I was a little tadpole. In the swamp where I grew up, there was always someone to play with, and we loved to hop and jump and splash. (We especially loved to splash!) When I got older I was lucky enough to travel all over the world, and I met and played with lots of kids in all the amazing places I visited. By the time I'd jumped rope in seventeen countries, climbed trees from Germany to Guatemala, and played tag from Mongolia to Mexico, one thing was clear: It didn't matter what language kids spoke or what clothes they wore, they all loved to play just as much as I did. So what are you waiting for? Call a friend, pick up a toy, or just bring your imagination. It's time to come out and play!

Kermit the Frog

Kermit the Frog © and ™ The Jim Henson Company

To play means swinging

Rocking back and forth in Egypt

Swinging on a
rope in Nepal

and jumping

Hopping in a sack race in the United States

Leaping through flowers on a kibbutz in Israel

and running

*Playing tag
in Mexico*

Running a race in Nicaragua

and climbing.

Climbing up a homemade
ladder in Norway

*Hanging on bars
in Jamaica*

To play means tossing and catching

Throwing a ball in Egypt

Playing baseball in the Dominican Republic

and hitting and kicking balls.

*Going after a ball
in the United States*

*Kicking a soccer
ball in Costa Rica*

To play means using your toys

Playing with a truck in Senegal

Walking on stilts in Thailand

Playing a string game in Egypt

Riding a tricycle in the Dominican Republic

Speeding down a hill in the United States

and using your imagination.

Pretending to be a farmer in the United States

Loving a doll in Kenya

Caring for a make-believe baby in Spain

To play means creating things

Painting a papier-mâché dragon in Australia

Building with blocks in the United States

and making things fly.

Flying a kite in Puerto Rico   . . . and in China

Blowing bubbles in Mexico

You can play inside

Playing a card game in Japan

Practicing gymnastics in Russia

and outside,

Going for a hike in the United States

Playing with grass
in Mongolia

Ice-skating in Sweden

at a playground

Riding seesaws in Peru

Swinging in Hungary

Rocking on a horse in Oman

or an amusement park.

*Spinning on a
Ferris wheel in India*

*Riding a carousel in
the United States*

You can play in the water

Cooling off in the United States

Floating in a stream in Thailand

Splashing around in France

and on the water.

*Paddling a canoe
in Guatemala*

*Wading and
sliding across
ice in Canada*

You can play all kinds of games.

Winning a computer game in the United States

Playing jacks in Honduras

Competing at foosball in Bolivia

Chasing a friend in a game of catch-the-wolf in Canada

You can play in all kinds of places.

Climbing a tree in
the Philippines

Flipping off a dock in Belize

Learning chess at a park in the United States

Playing cards in an alley in Brazil

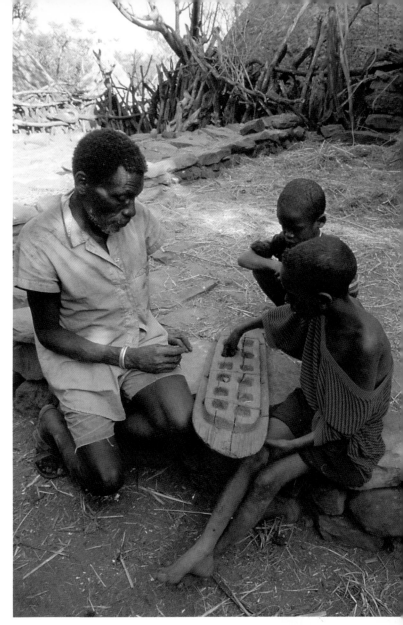

Playing bao in the yard in Ethiopia

You can play on your own

Making string figures
in French Polynesia

Rolling a hoop
in Nicaragua

Driving a
go-cart
in China

and with your friends.

Dancing in Lebanon

Enjoying furry friends in Tibet

To play means having lots and lots of fun.

Practicing for a baseball game in Guam

Aiming rubber bands at a target in Thailand

Jumping rope in Ethiopia

Floating on an inner tube in the United States

ALL KINDS OF TOYS

Almost anything can be a toy. A toy can be a truck you make from wire or a house you build from a cardboard box. Jump ropes, hoops, stilts, kites, and balls are toys found all over the world. Sometimes you use your toys by yourself and sometimes you share them with your friends. What is your favorite toy?

China

PLACES TO PLAY

You can play anywhere and everywhere. Swinging, jumping, running, and climbing often need wide-open spaces. Other types of play are best done inside, especially when the weather is rainy or cold. Amusement parks and playgrounds are special places to have great fun. But sometimes your backyard or your kitchen can be the best place of all.

United Kingdom

LOTS OF GAMES

There are many kinds of games. Checkers, chess, and go fish are games in which you try to be more clever than the other players. Tag, Ping-Pong, catch-the-wolf, and hide-and-seek are games in which speed and coordination are very important. Cooperation and teamwork are a big part of lots of games, from putting together puzzles to playing baseball or hockey. What is your favorite game?

Burkina Faso

USING YOUR IMAGINATION

Everything is new when you use your imagination. It lets you travel to distant lands, make new friends, build wonderful things, and enjoy exciting adventures. When you pretend to be a farmer, an explorer, or a mother or father, you are creating a world that is all your own.

France

Bulgaria

MAKING FRIENDS

Play brings friends together around the world. Whether you are working together, competing against each other, or just goofing off, friends help make play fun. Joking around and making silly faces bring lots of laughter. Sharing toys, joining in games, and spending time together help friendships grow into something that can last a lifetime. Can you come out and play?

For the children of the Train Platform Schools in Bubeneshwar, India
—M. A.

For the "seventh generation of children on earth"
—J. I.

I wish to thank my ever-cheering wife, Lisa Kivirist, and Cass DuRant, who opened her home in D.C. to me during the creation of this book. It has been a wonderful creative partnership to work with Maya Ajmera and to share in her vision for what the world can become, one child at a time.   *—John Ivanko*

As always, my deepest thanks to John Ivanko.   *—Maya Ajmera*

We would both like to thank our fantastic editors, Kelly Swanson Turner and Lisa Laird; Charlesbridge Publishing; Cheryl Henson, Susan Kantor, Tricia Boczkowski, Jane Leventhal, and Lauren Attinello of the Jim Henson Company; and Derek Brown of Ashoka, Innovators for the Public.

Financial support for this project has been provided by the W. K. Kellogg Foundation and the Flora Family Foundation.

Come Out and Play is a project of SHAKTI for Children, which is dedicated to teaching children to value diversity and to grow into productive and caring citizens of the world. SHAKTI for Children is a program of the Global Fund for Children, a non-profit organization. Visit www.globalfundforchildren.org to learn more about the Train Platform Schools.

Text copyright © 2001 by SHAKTI for Children
Photographs copyright © 2001 by individual copyright holders
Foreword copyright © 2001 The Jim Henson Company
KERMIT THE FROG is a trademark of The Jim Henson Company.
All rights reserved.

All rights reserved, including the right of reproduction in whole or in part in any form.

Published by Charlesbridge Publishing
85 Main Street, Watertown, MA 02472
(617) 926-0329 • www.charlesbridge.com

Developed by SHAKTI for Children
The Global Fund for Children
1612 K Street N.W., Suite 706, Washington, DC 20006
(202) 331-9003 • www.shakti.org

Details about donation of royalties can be obtained by writing to Charlesbridge Publishing and the Global Fund for Children.

Other SHAKTI for Children/Charlesbridge Books
Children from Australia to Zimbabwe: A Photographic Journey around the World by Maya Ajmera and Anna Rhesa Versola (1997)
Extraordinary Girls by Maya Ajmera, Olateju Omolodun, and Sarah Strunk (1999)
Let the Games Begin! by Maya Ajmera and Michael J. Regan (2000)
To Be a Kid by Maya Ajmera and John Ivanko (1999)
Xanadu, the Imaginary Place: A Showcase of Writings and Artwork by North Carolina's Children edited by Maya Ajmera and Olateju Omolodun (1999)

Library of Congress Cataloging-in-Publication Data
Ajmera, Maya.
Come out and play/Maya Ajmera and John Ivanko.
    p.   cm.
        ISBN 1-57091-385-4 (reinforced for library use)
        ISBN 1-57091-386-2 (softcover)
1. Play—Juvenile literature. [1. Play. 2. Games.] I. Ivanko, John D. (John Duane), 1966- . II. Shakti for Children (Organization). III. Title.
GV182.9.A56   2001
790—dc21   00-038371

Printed in South Korea
(hc) 10 9 8 7 6 5 4 3 2 1
(sc) 10 9 8 7 6 5 4 3 2 1

Display type and text type set in Jacoby, Stone Serif, and Stone Sans
Scans produced by ARTSLIDES, Somerville, Massachusetts
Color separations made by Sung In Printing, South Korea
Printed and bound by Sung In Printing, South Korea
Production supervision by Brian G. Walker
Designed by Diane M. Earley

Photographs: (counter-clockwise from top left): Cover: © John Russell/ Network Aspen; Front Flap: © Jon Warren; Title Page: © Jon Warren; pp. 2-3: © The Jim Henson Company, © John D. Ivanko; pp. 4-5: © Nick Wheeler, © Jon Warren, © Richard T. Nowitz; © Nick Wheeler; pp. 6-7: © Robert Frerck/ Woodfin Camp, © Jon Warren, © Nicki Mathias, © Jan Reynolds; pp. 8-9: © Monkmeyer/ Bopp, © Nick Wheeler, © Monkmeyer/ Collins, © John Russell/ Network Aspen; pp. 10-11: © Steven Herbert, © Nick Wheeler, © Peter Hammond/ Network Aspen, © Monkmeyer, © Nick Wheeler; pp. 12-13: © John D. Ivanko, © Monkmeyer/ Grantpix, © Patricia K. Sereduck; © John D. Ivanko; pp. 14-15: © Stephanie Maze, © Bill Bachmann/ Network Aspen, © Press/ Woodfin Camp, © Jeffrey Aaronson/ Network Aspen, © Yamashita/ Woodfin Camp; pp. 16-17: © Richard T. Nowitz, © Monkmeyer/ Siteman, © Elaine Little; © John Russell/ Network Aspen, © Jan Reynolds; pp. 18-19: © Monkmeyer/ Conklin, © Jon Warren, © Nick Wheeler, © Michele Burgess, © Monkmeyer/ Forsyth; pp. 20-21: © John Russell/ Network Aspen, © Monkmeyer/ Rogers, © Nick Wheeler, © Momatiuk/ Eastcott/ Woodfin Camp, © Curt Carnemark/World Bank; pp. 22-23: © Jennifer Davis, © Sean Sprague, © Jon Warren, © Jan Reynolds; pp. 24-25: © John D. Ivanko, © Nick Wheeler, © Sean Sprague, © Michele Burgess, © Nick Wheeler; pp. 26-27: © Jon Warren, © Victor Englebert, © Nick Wheeler, © Jeffrey Aaronson/ Network Aspen, © Katrina Thomas/ Aramco World; pp. 28-29: © Jon Warren, © Nick Wheeler, © Michele Burgess, © John Russell/ Network Aspen; pp. 30-31: © Jeffrey Aaronson/ Network Aspen, © Nick Wheeler, © Jon Warren, © Sean Sprague, © Monkmeyer/ Baum; Back Cover: © John Russell/ Network Aspen.